# The Tears That Water My Growth

Aria Amos

Copyright © 2024 Aria Amos

All rights reserved. In accordance with U.S. Copyright Act of 1976, the scanning, uploading, and electronic sharing of any part of this book without permission of the publisher constitute unlawful piracy and theft of the author's intellectual property. No part of this book may be reproduced in any form by any electronic or mechanical means (including photocopying, recording or information storage and retrieval) without permission in writing from the author or publisher. Thank you for your support of the author's rights.

Published by Richter Publishing LLC
[www.richterpublishing.com](www.richterpublishing.com)

Book Cover Design: Jessie Alarcon

Editors: Austin Hatch, Abigail Bunner & Elizabeth Pottinger

Additional Contributors: Tara Richter

Illustrations: Molly McGreevy

Book Formatting: Austin Hatch

ISBN-13: 978-1-954094-57-4

# DISCLAIMER

This book is a work of poetry. This information is provided and sold with the knowledge that the publisher and author do not offer any legal or medical advice. In the case of a need for any such expertise consult with the appropriate professional. This book does not contain all information available on the subject. This book has not been created to be specific to any individual people or organizations' situation or needs. Reasonable efforts have been made to make this book as accurate as possible. However, there may be typographical and or content errors. Therefore, this book should serve only as a general guide and not as the ultimate source of subject information. This book contains information that might be dated or erroneous and is intended only to educate and entertain. The author and publisher shall have no liability or responsibility to any person or entity regarding any loss or damage incurred, or alleged to have incurred, directly or indirectly, by the information contained in this book or as a result of anyone acting or failing to act upon the information in this book. You hereby agree never to sue and to hold the author and publisher harmless from any and all claims arising out of the information contained in this book. You hereby agree to be bound by this disclaimer, covenant not to sue and release. You may return this book within the guarantee time period for a full refund. All characters appearing in this work have given permission. Any resemblance to other real persons, living or dead is purely coincidental. The opinions in this work are purely of the author and not that of the publisher.

# DEDICATION

I am dedicating this book to my parents: my mum, Rachel Amos, and my dad, Anthony Amos. They are the reason I am where I am today. With the lessons they have taught me and the love they gave me, they have helped me see life through a completely different lens. My parents were the best parents I could've ever asked for, and although they have passed away, they are the main inspiration for my poetry. They continue to live on through my thoughts and my words. They are with me every day, and words can never express how much they mean to me. I wake up every day thanking the universe for giving me the most beautiful examples of how a person should be. They had the most magnetic souls and not a day goes by where I don't think about them. Although they are gone, they will never be forgotten. I will love you forever, mum and dad.

## Table of Contents

*To grieve is the consequence of love* .................................................. 4
*1 MUM* .............................................................................................. 5
*2 GONE* ............................................................................................ 6
*3 TEARS THAT WATER MY GROWTH* ............................................. 7
*4 QUESTIONS* ................................................................................. 8
*5 STRANGERS* ................................................................................ 9
*6 BODY* .......................................................................................... 10
*7 NATURE* ..................................................................................... 11
*8 STUCK* ........................................................................................ 12
*9 GIFTS* ......................................................................................... 13
*10 PATIENCE* ................................................................................ 14
*11 SPACES* ................................................................................... 15
*12 AGES* ....................................................................................... 16
*13 DIRECTIONS* ........................................................................... 17
*14 DREAMS* ................................................................................. 18
*15 MATURITIES* ........................................................................... 19
*16 MEN* ........................................................................................ 20
*17 MUSIC* ..................................................................................... 21
*18 REMINDER* .............................................................................. 22
*19 MESSAGES* .............................................................................. 23
*20 CRAVING* ................................................................................ 24
*21 INSPIRATION* .......................................................................... 25
*22 DISTANCE* ............................................................................... 26
*23 MOON* ..................................................................................... 27
*24 HOME* ..................................................................................... 28
*25 SIGN* ........................................................................................ 29
*26 BLOOM* ................................................................................... 30
*27 GRATITUDE* ............................................................................. 31
*28 IDENTITY* ................................................................................. 32
*29 LOSS* ........................................................................................ 33
*30 CONFUSION* ........................................................................... 34
*31 BIRTHDAY* ............................................................................... 35
*32 THANK U* ................................................................................. 36
*33 GUIDANCE* .............................................................................. 37
*34 OFFSPRING* ............................................................................. 38
*35 THAT NIGHT* ........................................................................... 39
*36 WAR* ........................................................................................ 40
*37 PEACE* ..................................................................................... 41
*38 LOST* ........................................................................................ 42
*39 GUILT* ...................................................................................... 43

*40 CONTRADICTION*.................................................................*44*
*41 DEAR OCTOBER*...................................................................*45*
*42 FANTASY* ..............................................................................*46*
*43 EPIC LOVE STORY* ...............................................................*47*
*44 OVERGROWN*.....................................................................*48*
*45 LINENS* ................................................................................*49*
*46 WORDS* ...............................................................................*50*
*47 MOTHERHOOD* ..................................................................*51*
*48 CONNECTION* .....................................................................*52*
*49 SCARF*..................................................................................*53*
*50 CHILDHOOD* .......................................................................*54*
*51 GLASS*..................................................................................*55*
*52 GHOST* ................................................................................*56*
*53 PANDEMIC* ..........................................................................*57*
*54 LIE* .......................................................................................*58*
*55 BETRAYAL* ...........................................................................*59*
*56 BLAME* ................................................................................*60*
*57 WITNESSES* .........................................................................*61*
*58 FOUNDATION* ....................................................................*62*
*59 SILENCE*...............................................................................*63*
*60 BLESSING* ............................................................................*64*
*61 BROTHER* ............................................................................*65*
*62 CREATION* ...........................................................................*66*
*63 SIBLINGS* .............................................................................*67*
*64 LETTER* ................................................................................*68*
*65 VOICE*..................................................................................*69*
*66 DOG* ....................................................................................*70*
*67 WHAT SISTERHOOD MEANS TO ME...*................................*71*
*You're my little treasure.* ........................................................*72*
*68 MEMORIES*..........................................................................*73*
*69 STORY* .................................................................................*74*
*70 HERE* ...................................................................................*75*
*71 STAR*....................................................................................*76*
*72 FACE*....................................................................................*77*
*73 YOUR BED* ...........................................................................*78*
*I Love You To Pieces*................................................................*79*
*74 MYSTERY*.............................................................................*80*
*75 PARENTING*.........................................................................*81*
*76 MOVING* .............................................................................*82*
*77 MOVEMENT*........................................................................*83*
*78 TOUCH* ................................................................................*84*
*79 TROUBLE*.............................................................................*85*

*80 FURNITURE* ............................................................................. *86*
*81 COLD* ...................................................................................... *87*
*82 LAUGHTER IN ABSENCE* ............................................... *88*
*83 RELIABILITY*............................................................................ *89*
*84 GO* ............................................................................................. *90*
*85 GUESS*...................................................................................... *91*
*86 RE-INVENTING*..................................................................... *92*
*87 SANITY*..................................................................................... *93*
*88 MANTRA* ................................................................................. *94*
*89 SURVIVAL* ............................................................................... *95*
*90 HUMAN* .................................................................................. *96*
*91 PERFECTION* ......................................................................... *97*
*92 CYCLE*....................................................................................... *98*
*93 ENOUGH*................................................................................. *99*
*94 BOTTOM*................................................................................. *100*
*95 SYMBOL*.................................................................................. *101*
*96 SELF-LOVE* ............................................................................. *102*
*97 DESTINY*.................................................................................. *103*
*98 LOYALTY* ................................................................................ *104*
*99 PATTERN* ............................................................................... *105*
*100 DETAILS* ............................................................................... *106*
*101 NOW*...................................................................................... *107*
*102 TIME* ...................................................................................... *108*
*103 PERFECT* .............................................................................. *109*
*104 PUZZLE* ................................................................................. *110*
*105 BEAUTY* ................................................................................ *111*
*106 BORROW* ............................................................................. *112*
*107 WIND*..................................................................................... *113*
*108 CANCER* ............................................................................... *114*
*Closing Statement* ...................................................................... *116*

## ACKNOWLEDGMENTS

My siblings, Isabella and Austin Amos, have been by my side through everything. I truly don't know what I would have done without them. So, thank you for inspiring me every day, for giving me the strength to keep going, and for being a place to give all the love we have lost. They have truly been my biggest cheerleaders and I couldn't be more grateful. They have inspired me to finally take the leap and publish my writing and have always been people I can look to for advice. Without our parents, we have been each other's only family and have stuck together through thick and thin. So, thank you—your support has meant the world to me. You both mean so much and deserve all the good things that are coming your way.

# INTRODUCTION

I feel like I have lived so many lives, and I am only 18. I often reflect on all the things that have shaped me in my life, all the good and bad. I think about how much I have really been through and how much I have been able to experience. I owe it all to my parents. I have seen so many amazing places, and my beautiful parents have taught me a lot of important life lessons, such as never giving up, always giving back, living in the moment, trusting your gut, and always being grateful for what you have. These are just a few of the things they have taught not only me, but my two older siblings, Isabella and Austin Amos, through the years. Most importantly, they showed us what real love looks like. They taught us how important it is to stick together through everything, though we never knew how important that was until now. After traveling the country and settling down in New Hampshire, my dad got sick with cancer. If you knew him, you knew that, out of everything, cancer wouldn't be the thing to take him. He was so positive and didn't think for a second he wouldn't beat it. He always made it a priority to make someone's day, and you would always know if he was in the room: he lit it up every single time. He loved life more than anyone I knew. Later that year, he beat cancer like we all knew he would.

Then, my mum passed from medical malpractice. Our worlds shattered, especially my dad's. My mum was my best friend, and I will miss her forever. Her loss changed me, and a piece of me died with her that night. She was kind, gentle, and always knew how to have fun. Nothing could've ever prepared me for this. A week after she passed, my dad was re-diagnosed with cancer. This time it was ten times more aggressive. He fought so hard, but not even a year after my mum's passing, my dad died as well. My sister and I were his nurses and looked after him till the end. He died from cancer, but sometimes I think it was from a broken heart. My mum went into surgery a day after their 19th wedding anniversary, which was the 9th of October 2020, and my dad had said to her, "Next year will be better, Darls. I promise." He would always say that he shouldn't have waited to make it special, and how much he wished she could just come back. He passed away on the 2nd of October 2021, so I like to think that despite this horrible tragedy, they were still able to celebrate their 20th wedding anniversary together. I often think of this as an epic love story. They both lived to 49, were born in the same month and passed in the same month. Since then, we have had a lot of friends and family leave, have been homeless, have had no money and especially no parents to tell us how to handle everything. We have had to deal with immigration and having no family in the U.S., but despite all that, my siblings and I have had to do it all, and we have. On the other hand, we are so much stronger now and have had some pretty incredible people come into our lives, especially the few that stuck around through all of it. I tend to find the meaning in all things, especially these events. To say this has been the worst thing that has happened to me would be an understatement, but I wouldn't be able to handle it the way I have if it wasn't for the lessons they taught me. There is always sun after rain, and I just want to make my parents proud. So, I hope you can relate to my words in one way or another and that you can find some comfort in them. Despite the pain or struggle you are in right now; you will be OK.

*To grieve
is the consequence
of love*

## MUM

Those special memories of you will
Always bring a smile
If only I could have you back for a little while
Then we could sit and talk again
just like we used to do
You always meant so very much
and always will too
The fact that you're no longer here
will always cause me pain
But you're forever in my heart
Until we meet again

# GONE

Though you are not here in sight
You will forever hold my heart so tight
I miss your beautiful smile and I just wish you
Could come back for a while
So then I could hug you so tight and never let go
Which is what I wish I did a few weeks ago

## TEARS THAT WATER MY GROWTH

Salty like the pain I feel yet sweet
From the life we once had
The love lost and confused
Looking for a new home
Escaping by a water droplet
Filled with so much more than molecules
Filled with memories, pain, love
And hate
Making room and watering
New growth
It's time to let go

# QUESTIONS

Faith is my middle name
That holds a lot of pressure
It's hard to have faith when you've lost so much
When you've been screwed over time and time again
Thinking to yourself, "did this really happen?"
"All you need is faith" is a hard phrase to come by
when that's all you had
It didn't work
I trusted that my faith was strong enough
It wasn't, you died and I'm still here
Does that boil down to faith?
Was it my fault for not trying hard enough?
Was it just your time?
So many unanswered questions
Stuck in my head
Stuck on this page
Never answered
I'm angry and I miss you
I don't know what to believe but all I know is that
I love you

## STRANGERS

It's so refreshing that
You don't know me
My trauma
My story

I am just a normal girl
You don't have to be gentle
Or cautious

I am not my trauma
You see me how I used to
And for that I thank you

For someone who still
Recognizes that girl
Before the world shattered

You're mysterious and oblivious
Or am I just good at hiding things?

## BODY

My hands lost your touch
Just as much as my mind did
My hands lost the feeling of yours
My eyes lost the sight of your smile
My ears lost the sound of your voice
My soul was torn from yours
I'm sorry body— you deserve more

# NATURE

Nature shows us so many signs
I believe it is the connection between
Us and our loved ones

The wind and rain
The timing of snow
Sunsets...
I think it's them
Putting on a show

They are around
Just keep your heart and mind open

Take a moment to be still amongst the chaos
To see what nature is trying to tell you
What they are trying to tell you

## STUCK

A roadblock
Not knowing how to put
My thoughts into words
I want to shake it all out
All the emotions, confused and lost
All the words I can't say to you
I guess it's just not right if I write
That I love you
And I miss you
And life isn't the same without you
And thank you
Thank you
Thank you
Because you will never read this
Never hear this
So, what does it matter?
I guess some words aren't worth saying
If the person you are saying them to
Isn't even here to listen

Or are they?

## GIFTS

One empath to another
You are doing amazing
The emotion you
Carry is powerful

# PATIENCE

Space is a strange
But beautiful thing
It is necessary but painful

Take your time
Give yourself the space you need

It is never selfish to listen
To yourself
Your mind
Your heart

## SPACES

Empty space in my heart
My soul
The spot you once claimed
The void that will never be whole

# AGES

Wrinkles on your face
You flinch, you "fix"
The wrinkles
Keeping track
Counting all the times you've smiled
Your skin keeping score

Your body a temple of
All the amazing things that have happened
So, you get rid of it
The natural beauty
Your soul cries
As you erase
The art of aging

# DIRECTIONS

I think nature teaches us a lot
About direction
The way the birds fly
Where the fish swim

It's been difficult for me
To feel like I am on the right path
Going in the right direction

Then I remember to trust the process
To listen to my intuition
That I will never fully
Know why or how
But to try to be more like
The birds and the fish
They seem to know
How to just let things flow

## DREAMS

I wake up just to sit there with
My eyes shut tight
Trying to remember my dream last night
Because I thought you were in it
To find any moment to hold onto you
For just a few more minutes

## MATURITIES

I'm trapped in my body
My mind three steps ahead
Shouting to slow down
But will never listen

Underestimated
Can't catch a break
Who ever said age
Was at stake?

"Adulting too young"
"Too young to adult"

Bite your tongue

# MEN

Why do you walk all over me
Using "women" as an insult
Always saying "it was your father's fault"
Men don't cry
Well neither do I
Did you ever really try?
You think you have all this power
Thinking you saved me
From that tower
My dad would be disappointed
He was a real man
Who never exploited

```
                                    MUSIC

                         I hear our song again
                              My heart sinks

                        The song I sang with you
                                  In the car
                                 At karaoke
                          On your hospital bed

                       A song that I will never
                           Hear the same again

                            Music heals the soul
                             But this one hurts
```

## REMINDER

Placing blame isn't healing
So start feeling all the feelings
Although it can be scary and
Feels like a lot to carry

You are capable
You have already come this far

## MESSAGES

In everything I see I try to find the meaning
You aren't a body with a soul
You are a soul with a body

Your skin is temporary
But your soul will never die

I can feel your presence
And I can see your messages
So keep sending them

I will always answer back

## CRAVING

Does this love hide
Away from me because
It is scared

Do I deserve this feeling
That I crave

Maybe it's better off
If you stay away

## INSPIRATION

You're gone, never coming back
You were the one that kept me on track
Your voice in my head
"Keep going"
So I do, for you
And hopefully for me one day too

## DISTANCE

We are looking at the same moon
Eyes glowing
Heart longing for you

To go back in time
To pretend nothing's changed

To love you again
To not feel so deranged

We are no longer aligned with the stars
Our hearts on different paths

## MOON

Looking at the moon
I wonder if you are looking too

HOME

Chatter in the kitchen
TV volume on one thousand
Sizzling on the stove
Laughter echoes

The house is full
We're all here
If only we knew death was near

The house alive
You alive
I miss the noise
I miss your voice

# SIGN

Little white butterflies
A sign filled with light
Your light
The one that made our house a home
The one that always had the insight

You find me when I need you most
Floating around
Is this your ghost?
You are always here for me
As you promised
You were always honest

Thank you for never turning
Off your light
A beacon for me
Even on the darkest of nights

## BLOOM

My heart blooms
For you
Making room
Pushing all the shit over
Just for you

Love heals but
Also avoids
Trying not to
Fill the void
That space will
Always be
For you

## GRATITUDE

Body fills with gratitude
My heart wants to explode

Letting the love in and
The hate go

```
IDENTITY
```

Are your emotions
The thing that defines you
Or is it a mask

I think "finding yourself"
Has become too much of a task
Making it a chore
Something to look for

When in reality it's
Right in front of you
All along here, now
Stop trying to find
Something that doesn't exist

You are perfect,
Authentic

# LOSS

The more I try to remember
The more I forget

Why do we hide memories?
To protect ourselves?

I tell myself I want to remember
But I think my mind is doing me a favor

The memories will always be there
We just have to be patient

## CONFUSION

Mind foggy
I try to keep my thoughts straight
But the flashbacks don't understand timing

I know I'm not there again
But it feels like I am

My heart races
I wonder how you felt

Suddenly I am back
To that night

The worst night of my life
And the end of yours
Mine ended a little too

My heart and mind are on
Different pages
Constantly playing catch up

# BIRTHDAY

Another year with you not here
Another year where I whisper
"Happy birthday" in hopes you'd hear

That phrase has never felt so silent

# THANK U

You have magic in those eyes
Deep blue magic
With hints of green

You knew me better than I did
Always seeing right through me
Healing me in ways you'll never know

Never let that magic go

## GUIDANCE

My thoughts in your voice
Always making a choice

The best advice
Never having to think twice

You knew what to say
And always gave me the choice
To choose which way

You helped me trust my own judgment
I will never forget it

# OFFSPRING

I am you
Your eyes
DNA
I love that you are a part of me
Forever

Through my heartbeat
Through my laugh
Everyone will know you
Mentioning you to everyone I meet

So every time I shed a tear
Know it's for the pure gratitude
That you are the reason I am here

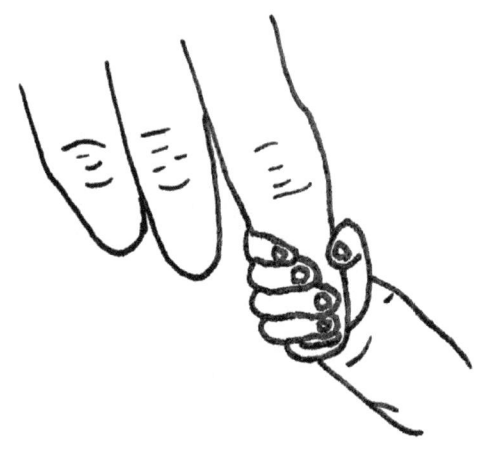

```
THAT NIGHT
```

My heart dropped
My world collapsed

I knew I was never going to be the same

# WAR

I am at war with myself
I am so angry
Why did this happen

I'm trying to be happy
Trying to live for you
It's exhausting

Why did you have to go
I'm torn between grief and gratitude

I am grateful for loving you
So deeply
But it hurts too much

The love lost
Seeping out of my pores
Searching for you
Longing for you

I am at war
I want the fight to end

Where are you to help me defend?

## PEACE

Breathe
Is it really worth it?
Protect your energy
Protect your peace

It will be ok

LOST

Am I still the girl you knew
You know the one
Before everything changed

The one that smiled
And meant it
The one that wasn't so on edge

Can you still hear her laugh
And see her smile

Can you help me find her again?

# GUILT

It creeps through my veins
Hides in my tears
Holding on to me so tight

Guilt
An emotion I can't understand
An emotion that is cruel
That blends in with all the others
Always overstaying
Its welcome

I blame myself for things I can't control
Things that were destined to be

Can I please just have control
Over one thing that happened to me?

## CONTRADICTION

Sacred to remember
But scared to forget

## DEAR OCTOBER

Why did you have to be so horrible
I love you but now you are intolerable
Leaves falling
Air changing
Memory so vivid
My feelings don't know what to do
They feel timid
Dear October,
Why did you have to take them away
All I asked for was for them to stay
Why do you never listen
It isn't fair
All I wanted was to see their smiles glisten
October you have been a tragedy
But I'll try to love you again
Because it wasn't your fault in reality

# FANTASY

I can't believe there are people
In this world that still think you are alive

How lucky are they

# EPIC LOVE STORY

We intertwined our fingers
Our souls
Attached for life
Heart beating for the other

Until it stopped

We are intertwined
Once again
Ash to ash
Soul to soul

Love lasts longer
Then just one lifetime

## OVERGROWN

The grief tangles around
My gratitude tree
Trying to wrap around its roots
Silently killing
The optimism
The love
So, I cut the weeds down
Knowing they will be back tomorrow
Appreciating the silence now

## LINENS

Your side of the bed
Your pillow
Your scent

I wanted to keep it warm
While you were gone

Little did I know
You were never coming back

Avoiding laundry day
Washing you away
Wishing you could stay

# WORDS

The more I bruise the page
The quicker something inside me heals

## MOTHERHOOD

We shared a heartbeat
Now mine beats for you

# CONNECTION

I just met you but our souls
Have known each other for a lifetime

Your words run up my spine
And ignite my brain
You get me

I don't need to explain the pain
I'm able to breathe I'm able
To grieve

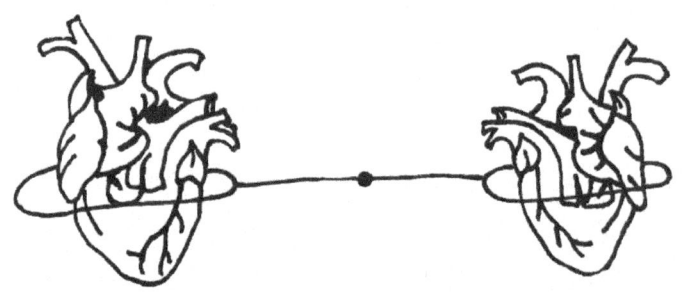

## SCARF

Your warm scarf wrapped around me
Like a blanket
The safest I will ever feel

# CHILDHOOD

Muffled voices echoing off the
Walls of the home we grew up in
Laughter and tired eyes
Whiskey breath whispering goodnight
Always sleeping tight

## GLASS

Glass half full
glass half empty
I wish you were with me
I am glad I still have water within me

## GHOST

I was no longer afraid of ghosts
After you became one

## PANDEMIC

Everyone wearing masks made me get to know your
eyes really well...

The light blue magic
With hints of yellow
Moon shapes when you smiled
Telling a million stories
Asking a million questions
With not a single answer
I knew when you weren't OK
The way puddles formed
And tears rolled
Like a beautiful sad melody
Your eyes were your worst enemy
Giving away all your secrets

```
LIE
```

My dreams keep lying to me
Please can I sleep in peace

## BETRAYAL

You walked away
But could I blame you
I would've too
My world was too blue

BLAME

Why am I punishing myself
Judging the emotions I can't control
Trying to fill this hole
It's not my fault or anyone's for that matter
It's life
People come and go

You will always have you
So be kind to her
Lean on her
You won't feel lost forever

# WITNESSES

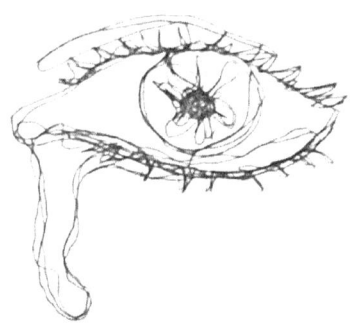

The guilt that piles
Wishing it was you
I feel vile

You're sick but
why do I feel sicker
It's not fair
It can't be true
That cancer got
The best of you

I am a witness to sickness
To death
The dark coldness
Stained on my skin
Feeling like I'll never win

What about me?
The doctors say I'm fine
But how can there be a prognosis
To this feeling like
I was touched by death too
Does this make me feel closer to you?

# FOUNDATION

My bones are strong like the roots that hold me together
No matter how much I fall
How much I fade
My roots will always remain the same

# SILENCE

My mind wanders again
All the way back to you
Regretting everything I ever said
I wish we could start over

Hi my name's Delusion,
What's yours again?

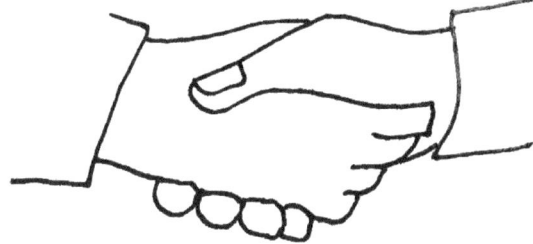

BLESSING

What a beautiful little life we live
Smiles from strangers
Honey tea on your sore throat
Hugging your mum after saying "I'm OK"
She knew you weren't
Love and heartache
Intuition, knowing we are all connected
What a blessing to walk this Earth
To breathe in the salty ocean air
The rain on hot pavement
The taste of tears for the first time
The support from your friends
To be a part of something so real
Yet so temporary
We are all in the same boat
Trying to navigate this beautiful scary world
You have so much to live for
No one has this life figured out
Thank you for staying
For just living
We need you

# BROTHER

My mum raised my brother right.
Always respect women, hold the door open,
Be protective, fill up the fuel,
Never swear around her, pay on the first date,
Bring her flowers, listen to her, pick her up,
Make her feel like she's the only girl in the world,
Be gentle, be patient, be kind,
Be a gentleman, always look out for your sisters,
Be strong and it's ok to cry, stop to help,
Step in when necessary and
Never love anyone more than your mum.

The men that were raised like my brother deserve the world.
We need more people like him.

CREATION

You created me
Your DNA is mine
My eyes are yours
What a gift
To know I am from you
To know I was once you
You took care of me
Watched me grow
Until it was your time to go
Nurtured me into the person I am
Someone I'll always know
I am proud to be your little creation

# SIBLINGS

You have known me since birth
Longer than I have been on this Earth

We were kids together
Laughed together
Saw snow for the first time together

Witnessed Dad cry together
Hearts heavy
Smiles wide together
Hugged Mum goodbye together
Eyes cried
Hearts ripped open together

Always sticking together

# LETTER

I write and erase
Write and erase
No words will make you stay
What would I even say
Would you write back anyway

## VOICE

Your voice like an angel
Soft and sweet
Always bringing the tears out of me

## DOG

You are pure
Shielded from all the bad things this life offers
You love unconditionally
Forgive with no doubt
Comfort like you know the pain
Maybe you do get it
I wonder if you could talk
Would you tell me all of life's secrets
Tell me how you do it
How to live without a care in the world

# WHAT SISTERHOOD MEANS TO ME...

Having someone to call home
A person that is brave and beautiful
Someone to look up to
To tell my secrets to
A person to lean on
Bleeding the same blood
Never having to explain
And never feeling ashamed
I'm always admiring her beauty
Her strength
A girl that is now a woman
With beautiful blue eyes
That I know so well
A beautiful soul with stories to tell
We grieve together and laugh together
Bread from the same dough
All that lost love having somewhere to go.

*You're my little treasure.*

## MEMORIES

Cherish the little moments
I promise they won't be little forever

STORY

Who would I be without you
How would my story go
I'm glad I'll never know

## HERE

You are fully in control
You create your reality
Have a little more faith in yourself

## STAR

We lay there stargazing
Naming our favourite stars
You name one after me
The brightest one
You say how much we have in common
I smiled
You stared
I see a shooting star
So do you
We scream and go silent
Knowing we are both making wishes
Mine never came true
I know we don't talk anymore
But did yours never too?
Maybe it was just a faulty star

## FACE

I memorize your face
The tears you are trying to hide
The love you are confused to carry
The way you flinch at affection
But melt with him
You are strong
But you are struggling
All knowing but lost
Like the ships at sea
He is your lighthouse
The one that brings you to shore
He is also the tide that pushes you back

# YOUR BED

I had a bad dream
I squish in between you and Dad
Counting sheep till I fall asleep

First day of second grade
I run upstairs and tell you about my day
You say how proud you are
I fall asleep in your arms

Year 9
You pick me up early
I asked you to
We got lunch and you asked if I was OK
You always listened
We got home and watched our favourite show

Year 10
You died
I sleep in your spot next to Dad
Not saying anything but our souls communicating
Feeling each other's loss
They could relate

Year 11
I thought I had a bad dream
Dad died except it wasn't a dream this time
I lay in the middle squished between the bodies that once lay there
Counting sheep
Wishing I could just fall asleep
And this was all just a dream

*I*
   *Love*
      *You*
         *To*
            *Pieces*

# MYSTERY

Just like that we are strangers again
You knew me
I let you in
You knew the colour of my eyes
And the feeling of my hair
But did you ever listen
When I told you my favourite memories
Or the weight that my heart carries
Did you watch when I showed you my tenderness
Or only If I got undressed
Was I just another body to you?
A mystery
I should've known your game
Your trickery

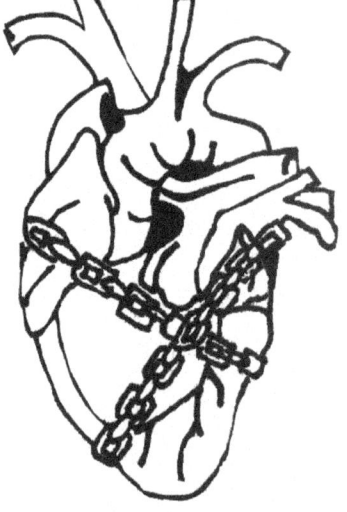

## PARENTING

You raised me to know my worth
Ever since birth
But I grew up
And realized personality is never enough
They judge and critique
Until I become bleak
It took over
I hate on my face
The one that you tried so hard to create

I think about it that way
I am your creation
From your mutation
Something you left behind
Just in time

So it's not fair to shit on
Your art
Your legacy
So I will look past the jealousy
And admire your masterpiece

I will look in the mirror to see you
Hoping you are looking down to see me too

```
MOVING
```

Moving into a new house without you
Feels too new
Feels too blue

I got comfortable
Or at least used to
Living with your ghost
In the home where you lived
In the bed where you slept

I could look in the kitchen
Where you once cooked
I could play pretend
As if nothing ever happened

I can't play pretend here
This house doesn't know you
This floor doesn't know your footsteps
These walls haven't felt the echo of your laugh

Hasn't felt the weight of you being gone
The grief settling in like the floorboards

## MOVEMENT

Soulmates
The movement of two souls
Longing for each other
Moving together
Even when they are apart
Except in this poem, they never meet
They settle for less
Never feeling sound
Some soulmates are never found

TOUCH

I forgot what your touch feels like
What your voice sounds like

So I sit and I think
Trying to remember all the memories

Reminding me why
I feel this way all the time
Remember that you're the
Reason I have this hole inside

I have all this love to give
To a ghost
Because I always knew
I loved you the most

Constantly thinking
That maybe in another life
You didn't have to die

## TROUBLE

This grief is in my blood
My heart sinks
Constantly on the run
I feel like I can't breathe
Tangles around my lungs

It's with me everywhere I go
Waiting to strike
Feeling like it's the only thing I know

It's scared because it doesn't have a home
No place to go
This feeling is lost love
But I find myself feeling lost too

I miss you
And this grief is a reminder
I will learn to live with it
Because it helps me hold onto
You a little tighter

FURNITURE

This lounge that I sit on
Holds your scent
Remembers your laugh
Fit to your body
It's witnessed my tears
Held me on my worst nights
It is worn and has tears
But I can't let it go

It holds memories
All the good
All the bad
It knows me
Knows us

Or at least what we used to be

# COLD

I'm cold
The grief like ice
Numbing every part of me
My palms are sweating
But I'm shivering
Your body like a beam of sunlight
Warming me even at night
And throughout the day
I feel like the Earth if the Sun was taken away

You were my Sun

# LAUGHTER IN ABSENCE

Your laughter sounds different
Now that she's gone
Your sad eyes consistent
Your fake smile always on

She was your muse
And you were hers too

Two souls intertwined
In every lifetime

# RELIABILITY

You hugged me so tight
As if you'd never let go
Your fingers through my hair
Lying on the same pillow
You got up to leave
Kissed me on the cheek
If only I knew this was a one-time thing

## GO

Feel the Sun on your face
And the breeze through your hair
Smile at the wildflowers
And lay on the grass

Stargaze and cloud watch
Let go
Because you never know
When each breath is your last
So hold this life tight
And grasp all the beauty

You might just see that each day is worth living
So do all the things that make you smile
And live in this moment right now
For a while

## GUESS

Guessing what you said
Thinking what you thought
Making up scenarios
That leave me so distraught

Did you even think?
Did you ever care?
Or was I this delusional
To think there was something there

# RE-INVENTING

I'm not a stranger to my laugh anymore
Nor am I a stranger to my cry

I love myself
Or at least I try

I don't rely on you anymore
To help me be ok
I don't feel so numb
Nor do I constantly re-live that day

I am healing
In more ways than one
And although it's not linear
I am alive and I can feel the sun

So when you ask
"Are you ok?"
I will say
"I will be. Just taking it day by day."

## SANITY

I can't remember the last
Time I took a deep breath

When you left
You took so much of me with you
You took the sparkle in my eye
You took my laugh
You even took my cry

I feel numb
Like all that's left is a shell
Where you once lived

They say to never love
Someone else more than yourself
But I didn't listen

Maybe you just outgrew this place
Outgrew me
But what's even worse
Is I'd take you back in a heartbeat

## MANTRA

Integrity, courage, honor
The 3 words repeated in childhood
3 words that aren't said enough
Respected enough
Where did decency go?
Morals go?
What do those 3 words mean
Because it seems like no one knows

## SURVIVAL

All the emotions suppressed by fight or flight
Came into my dreams last night
Emotions I always fight
Because what happened will never be alright

# HUMAN

You are the stream
Constantly flowing
Changing, evolving
You are the beam
The light that's always showing
So let the river flow
And let the light shine
Everything that's meant to be, will be
With time

## PERFECTION

I wish you felt the way I did
I wish you never hid
From this spark
The feeling that made everything
A little less dark

We could've been something you know
But you had different plans for your show
I was just a stepping stone
But you
You were someone I thought I could get to know

# CYCLE

I let you in when
I knew I was just
Another girl on the roster

Getting heartbroken
Thinking this is a shocker
I knew it but I still
Gave you so much to offer

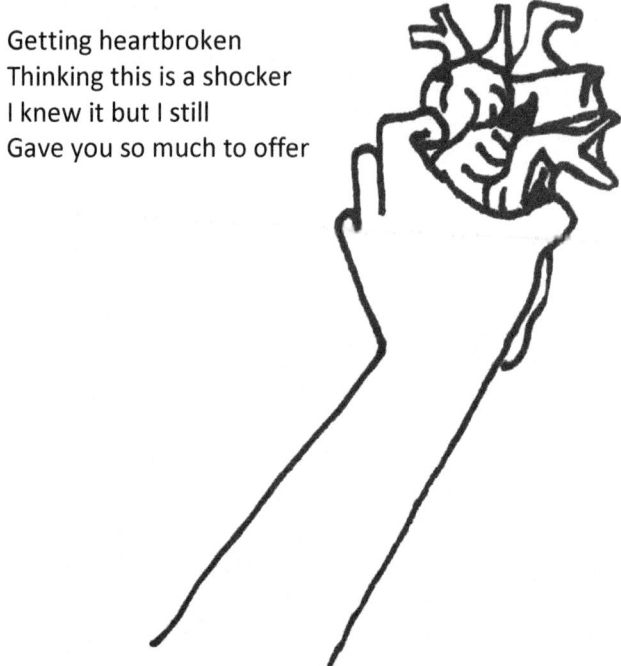

## ENOUGH

Your heartbeat gave it away
I could feel it race
As my fingers traced your face

So why lie
Why hide
Why did you keep all your feelings inside

BOTTOM

Hitting rock bottom
Seeing no light
Wishing for the flowers to blossom
Trying so hard to fight

But know it will be alright
There is only one way
So don't give up
Because one day
You'll look back
And see how important it was to stay

## SYMBOL

A blue dragonfly
I know it's you
I feel your energy as it flies by

My oh my
Do I wish I could fly

```
SELF-LOVE
```

I want to climb out of my skin
Out of this body
This body that has been
Spread too thin
This body that went through hell
That fell and still got up
That's bruised and scarred
That never gave up

I want to love my skin
Thank my body
For being here for me
Through thick and thin
I want to embody
All the love she always gives
I want to be grateful
Because she's the reason I live

# DESTINY

I know nothing's permanent
But gosh I wish you were

## LOYALTY

You saw through my mask
Through all the tasks
The ones I use to distract

You saw me clearly
And did not leave me
You stayed
And for that
I will thank you every day

## PATTERN

It's a pattern
They come
They take
They leave
Until there is nothing
Left of me

```
DETAILS
```

It's the little details
The way the sky looked
The crisp air through my hair
The taste of my salty tears
Wishing I didn't hear
That you will no longer be near

## NOW

Just be still and open
To living in the moment

# TIME

Time heals all things
People move on

# PERFECT

Like perfect pieces
Always completing the other

## PUZZLE

The great puzzle of life
Picking up pieces as you go
Some never fitting no matter
How hard you try
You push and you jam
Until it breaks
You move on
Sometimes never feeling like
The puzzle will be complete
But remember you will
Always find the final piece

# BEAUTY

I am from butterfly kisses
And intuition
From love and light
From late nights
I am from the moon
And the tides
From looking in the eye
I am from never give up
And trust your gut
I am from grief
From saying goodbye
At the worst times
I am from gratitude
And always looking for signs

## BORROW

I gave you my heart to borrow
You said I will see you tomorrow
You never returned
Now I am left here to burn

# WIND

Why is the wind beautiful?

It brings leaves to places they have never been
It lets trees hug
It helps birds fly
It brings life to new places
Places new life

## CANCER

We thought you were healthy
But cancer is stealthy
Like a robber in the night
Always putting up a good fight

# Closing Statement

I am on a mission to help others feel heard in their journey of grief. I have been writing poetry for about four years now. I started when my mum passed away. The grief was heavy, and writing seemed to make it feel a little lighter. A little under a year later, I lost my dad, and I still turned to poetry. It has been an outlet in a way for me, a place to write down all the words and feelings I can't express to them anymore. Grief is confusing yet beautiful. I have experienced a lot of it in my life, but it has made me grow in ways I never thought I could. I am doing it, navigating through life after going through something so difficult. This is not to say I don't think about them every day or that this has been easy in any aspect, but I am here, and that's what matters. After my mum passed, I didn't know what to do. I was feeling emotions I had never felt before and was having full-blown panic attacks almost every day. My dad helped me a lot with that because he could relate. So, I started writing poetry. Every chance I got I would sit and just let the words and my feelings flow. Now I have written this book to show that despite the weight of grief, anxiety, depression, and all the feelings that come up, it is OK. I know it's said all the time, but it really is. You can go through hard things and find joy on the other side. My mum often said, "If you can't, you must," and that's what I did. I thought there was no way I could live the rest of my life without them, especially losing them so young, but I have. Not just for them, but for me too. To appreciate how temporary life can be and how important it is to be here now. Every day I think to myself, "what would they do?" and the answer is— they would keep going. Grief is something I will never fully understand, and I will miss them forever, but every day I am finding out more about myself. How to let my emotions flow and how to understand my mind better. To know that it is OK to feel so sad or to even feel happy. To know that your emotions are going to come up and to just let them. So, I hope you can find some peace in my words, to know that there is light at the end of the tunnel and that everything is going to work out.

Mum and dad,

I will love you forever. Thank you

# ABOUT THE AUTHOR

My name is ARIA Amos. The reason my name is capitalized is because it is the first initial of each of my family members' names. My dad Anthony, my mum Rachel, my sister Isabella and my brother Austin. I am the youngest of my family and I am proud to say my name because it comes from the people that have shaped me into the person I am today. My family inspires me, and the lessons my parents have taught me have impacted my life for the better. I have had a very interesting life in my short 18 years. I am from Australia and have moved to the United States with my parents and two siblings. We moved here in 2011 and have been back and forth since. I have lived most of my life in the U.S., but Australia will always be my home. I have travelled to 48 states in the United States to raise money and awareness for animal rescue. My parents owned a mobile dog grooming unit, HydroDog, that we'd take to shelters and events to wash dogs. One hundred percent of the proceeds we made would go straight back to whichever shelter we were raising money for that day. I was the dog washer with my brother, and although it was really hard work, it was worth it. I was taught the value of giving back at a really young age, and it has impacted my life forever. Seeing the dogs I had just washed from the shelter get adopted would make my day and is something that I will always look back on. After travelling for about three years, Animal Planet asked if we wanted to do a TV show on the work we had been doing. We said yes and started filming soon after. The film crew followed us around for about three months, and that was one of the most memorable experiences I have had yet. The show is called" Furever Home Family" on Animal Planet, and I will always be so grateful to my parents for giving me all these amazing experiences. I have always believed in the universe and how important it is to be impeccable with your words. How you are in control of your thoughts and your destiny. I believe that there is always room for growth, and I know from experience how beautiful that growth can be. After losing both my parents, I have learnt a lot about myself.

www.ingramcontent.com/pod-product-compliance
Lightning Source LLC
Chambersburg PA
CBHW070313010526
44107CB00004B/322